Little Budget Book

Little Budget Book

This planner belongs to:

_____

If found, please contact:

_____

Turn that dream
into a plan

FINANCIAL GOALS

GOAL ONE

ACTION STEPS   NOTES

DUE BY:

GOAL TWO

ACTION STEPS   NOTES

DUE BY:

FINANCIAL GOALS

GOAL THREE

ACTION STEPS

NOTES

DUE BY:

GOAL FOUR

ACTION STEPS

NOTES

DUE BY:

INVESTMENTS

SUPERANNUATION

Fund	Contributions	Balance

GOALS

STOCKS

Company	Buy/Sell	Qty	Price	Fees	Total

OTHER

INVESTMENT VALUE:

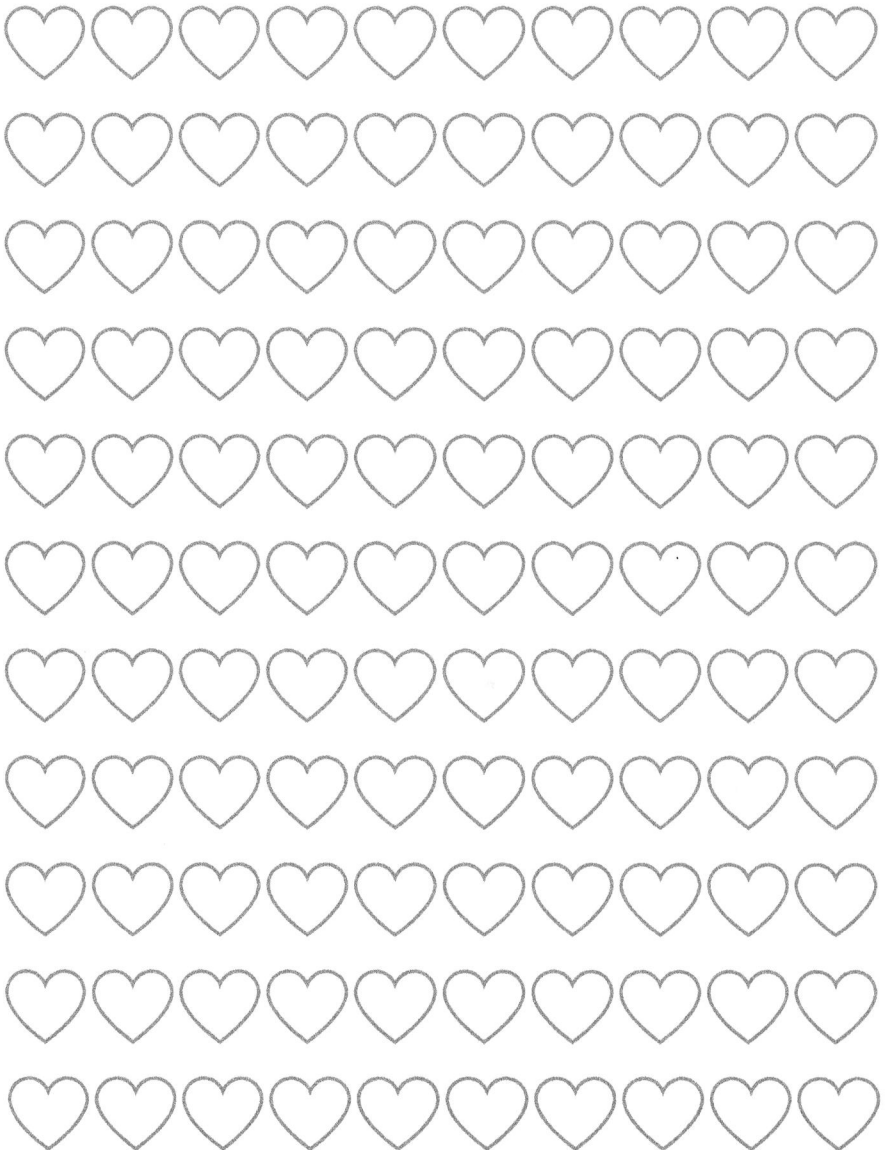

SAVINGS TRACKER

FUND:

EACH HEART EQUALS:

GOAL:

♡ ♡ ♡ ♡ ♡ ♡ ♡ ♡ ♡ ♡

♡ ♡ ♡ ♡ ♡ ♡ ♡ ♡ ♡ ♡

♡ ♡ ♡ ♡ ♡ ♡ ♡ ♡ ♡ ♡

♡ ♡ ♡ ♡ ♡ ♡ ♡ ♡ ♡ ♡

♡ ♡ ♡ ♡ ♡ ♡ ♡ ♡ ♡ ♡

♡ ♡ ♡ ♡ ♡ ♡ ♡ ♡ ♡ ♡

♡ ♡ ♡ ♡ ♡ ♡ ♡ ♡ ♡ ♡

♡ ♡ ♡ ♡ ♡ ♡ ♡ ♡ ♡ ♡

♡ ♡ ♡ ♡ ♡ ♡ ♡ ♡ ♡ ♡

♡ ♡ ♡ ♡ ♡ ♡ ♡ ♡ ♡ ♡

♡ ♡ ♡ ♡ ♡ ♡ ♡ ♡ ♡ ♡

SAVINGS TRACKER

FUND:

GOAL AMOUNT

EACH PIGGY =

MINDMAP

WAYS I CAN MAKE MORE/SAVE MORE

DEBT REPAYMENTS

DESCRIPTION	BALANCE	INTEREST RATE	MIN. PAYMENT

NOTES

FREQUENCY	EXTRA PAYMENTS	TARGET PAY OFF DATE

BILLS

BILL	AMOUNT	DUE	FREQUENCY

BILLS

BILL	AMOUNT	DUE	FREQUENCY

SUBSCRIPTIONS

SUBSCRIPTION	AMOUNT	DUE	FREQUENCY

IMPORTANT DATES

JANUARY

FEBRUARY

MARCH

APRIL

MAY

JUNE

JULY

AUGUST

SEPTEMBER

OCTOBER

NOVEMBER

DECEMBER

MONTH OF

GOALS	MONDAY	TUESDAY	WEDNESDAY
TARGET			
ACTUAL			
TARGET			
ACTUAL			
TARGET			
ACTUAL			

HABIT TRACKER

HABIT	1	2	3	4	5	6	7	8	9	10	11	12	13	14	15	16	17	18	19	20	21	22	23	24	25	26	27	28	29	30	31

THURSDAY	FRIDAY	SATURDAY	SUNDAY

NOTES

WEEKLY BUDGET

WEEK OF:

INCOME

Source	Estimated	Actual

SAVINGS

Account	Amount	+/-	Balance

DEBT

Description	Deposit	Balance

EXPENSES

Expense	Amount	Category

NOTES

WEEKLY

Total Income	
Total Debt	
Total Savings	
Total Expenses	

WEEKLY TO DO LIST

THIS WEEK'S FOCUS

TO DO LIST

PRIORITY

DUE

WEEK OF:

MONDAY	TUESDAY	WEDNESDAY	THURSDAY
MEALS	MEALS	MEALS	MEALS

PERSONAL TO DO LIST:

_____
_____
_____
_____
_____

WORK TO DO LIST:

_____
_____
_____
_____
_____

FRIDAY	SATURDAY	SUNDAY	THIS WEEK'S REMINDERS:
MEALS	MEALS	MEALS	

NOTES:

WEEKLY BUDGET

W E E K   O F :

INCOME

Source	Estimated	Actual

EXPENSES

Expense	Amount	Category

SAVINGS

Account	Amount	+/-	Balance

DEBT

Description	Deposit	Balance

NOTES

WEEKLY

Total Income	
Total Debt	
Total Savings	
Total Expenses	

WEEKLY TO DO LIST

THIS WEEK'S FOCUS

TO DO LIST

PRIORITY

DUE

WEEK OF:

MONDAY	TUESDAY	WEDNESDAY	THURSDAY
MEALS	MEALS	MEALS	MEALS

PERSONAL TO DO LIST:

_____
_____
_____
_____
_____

WORK TO DO LIST:

_____
_____
_____
_____
_____

FRIDAY	SATURDAY	SUNDAY
MEALS	MEALS	MEALS

_____
_____
_____
_____
_____
_____
_____
_____
_____
_____
_____
_____
_____
_____
_____
_____
_____
_____
_____

NOTES:

WEEKLY BUDGET

WEEK OF:

INCOME

Source	Estimated	Actual

SAVINGS

Account	Amount	+/-	Balance

DEBT

Description	Deposit	Balance

WEEKLY

Total Income	
Total Debt	
Total Savings	
Total Expenses	

EXPENSES

Expense	Amount	Category

NOTES

WEEKLY TO DO LIST

TO DO LIST

PRIORITY

DUE

WEEK OF:

MONDAY	TUESDAY	WEDNESDAY	THURSDAY
MEALS	MEALS	MEALS	MEALS

PERSONAL TO DO LIST:

_____
_____
_____
_____
_____
_____

WORK TO DO LIST:

_____
_____
_____
_____
_____
_____

FRIDAY	SATURDAY	SUNDAY	THIS WEEK'S REMINDERS:
MEALS	MEALS	MEALS	

NOTES:

WEEKLY BUDGET

WEEK OF:

INCOME

Source	Estimated	Actual

SAVINGS

Account	Amount	+/-	Balance

DEBT

Description	Deposit	Balance

WEEKLY

Total Income	
Total Debt	
Total Savings	
Total Expenses	

EXPENSES

Expense	Amount	Category

NOTES

WEEKLY TO DO LIST

THIS WEEK'S FOCUS

TO DO LIST	PRIORITY

DUE

WEEK OF:

MONDAY	TUESDAY	WEDNESDAY	THURSDAY
MEALS	MEALS	MEALS	MEALS

PERSONAL TO DO LIST:

_____
_____
_____
_____
_____

WORK TO DO LIST:

_____
_____
_____
_____
_____

FRIDAY	SATURDAY	SUNDAY
MEALS	MEALS	MEALS

THIS WEEK'S REMINDERS:

_____
_____
_____
_____
_____
_____
_____
_____
_____
_____
_____
_____
_____
_____
_____
_____
_____
_____
_____
_____
_____

NOTES:

GOALS UPDATE

MONTHLY OVERVIEW

SAVINGS

DEBT

WINS

CHALLENGES

NOTES

MONTH OF

GOALS	MONDAY	TUESDAY	WEDNESDAY
TARGET			
ACTUAL			
TARGET			
ACTUAL			
TARGET			
ACTUAL			

HABIT TRACKER

HABIT	1	2	3	4	5	6	7	8	9	10	11	12	13	14	15	16	17	18	19	20	21	22	23	24	25	26	27	28	29	30	31

THURSDAY	FRIDAY	SATURDAY	SUNDAY

NOTES

WEEKLY BUDGET

WEEK OF:

INCOME

Source	Estimated	Actual

SAVINGS

Account	Amount	+/-	Balance

DEBT

Description	Deposit	Balance

WEEKLY

Total Income	
Total Debt	
Total Savings	
Total Expenses	

EXPENSES

Expense	Amount	Category

NOTES

WEEKLY TO DO LIST

THIS WEEK'S FOCUS

TO DO LIST

PRIORITY

DUE

WEEK OF:

MONDAY	TUESDAY	WEDNESDAY	THURSDAY

MEALS   MEALS   MEALS   MEALS

PERSONAL TO DO LIST: WORK TO DO LIST:

_____   _____
_____   _____
_____   _____
_____   _____
_____   _____

FRIDAY	SATURDAY	SUNDAY	THIS WEEK'S REMINDERS:
MEALS	MEALS	MEALS	

NOTES:

WEEKLY BUDGET

WEEK OF:

INCOME

Source	Estimated	Actual

SAVINGS

Account	Amount	+/-	Balance

DEBT

Description	Deposit	Balance

WEEKLY

Total Income	
Total Debt	
Total Savings	
Total Expenses	

EXPENSES

Expense	Amount	Category

NOTES

WEEKLY TO DO LIST

THIS WEEK'S FOCUS

TO DO LIST

PRIORITY

DUE

WEEK OF:

MONDAY	TUESDAY	WEDNESDAY	THURSDAY
MEALS	MEALS	MEALS	MEALS

PERSONAL TO DO LIST:

_____
_____
_____
_____
_____

WORK TO DO LIST:

_____
_____
_____
_____
_____

FRIDAY	SATURDAY	SUNDAY
MEALS	MEALS	MEALS

_____
_____
_____
_____
_____
_____
_____
_____
_____
_____
_____
_____
_____
_____
_____
_____
_____
_____
_____
_____

NOTES:

WEEKLY BUDGET

WEEK OF:

INCOME

Source	Estimated	Actual

SAVINGS

Account	Amount	+/-	Balance

DEBT

Description	Deposit	Balance

WEEKLY

Total Income	
Total Debt	
Total Savings	
Total Expenses	

EXPENSES

Expense	Amount	Category

NOTES

WEEKLY TO DO LIST

TO DO LIST

PRIORITY

DUE

WEEK OF:

MONDAY	TUESDAY	WEDNESDAY	THURSDAY
MEALS	MEALS	MEALS	MEALS

PERSONAL TO DO LIST:

_____
_____
_____
_____
_____

WORK TO DO LIST:

_____
_____
_____
_____
_____

FRIDAY	SATURDAY	SUNDAY
MEALS	MEALS	MEALS

NOTES:

WEEKLY BUDGET

WEEK OF:

INCOME

Source	Estimated	Actual

SAVINGS

Account	Amount	+/-	Balance

DEBT

Description	Deposit	Balance

WEEKLY

Total Income	
Total Debt	
Total Savings	
Total Expenses	

EXPENSES

Expense	Amount	Category

NOTES

WEEKLY TO DO LIST

TO DO LIST

PRIORITY

DUE

WEEK OF:

MONDAY	TUESDAY	WEDNESDAY	THURSDAY
MEALS	MEALS	MEALS	MEALS

PERSONAL TO DO LIST:

_____
_____
_____
_____
_____

WORK TO DO LIST:

_____
_____
_____
_____
_____

FRIDAY	SATURDAY	SUNDAY	THIS WEEK'S REMINDERS:
MEALS	MEALS	MEALS	

NOTES:

GOALS UPDATE

MONTHLY OVERVIEW

SAVINGS   DEBT

WINS   CHALLENGES

NOTES

MONTH OF

GOALS	MONDAY	TUESDAY	WEDNESDAY
TARGET ACTUAL			
TARGET ACTUAL			
TARGET ACTUAL			

HABIT TRACKER

HABIT	1 2 3 4 5 6 7 8 9 10 11 12 13 14 15 16 17 18 19 20 21 22 23 24 25 26 27 28 29 30 31

THURSDAY	FRIDAY	SATURDAY	SUNDAY

NOTES

WEEKLY BUDGET

WEEK OF:

INCOME

Source	Estimated	Actual

SAVINGS

Account	Amount	+/-	Balance

DEBT

Description	Deposit	Balance

EXPENSES

Expense	Amount	Category

NOTES

WEEKLY

Total Income	
Total Debt	
Total Savings	
Total Expenses	

WEEKLY TO DO LIST

THIS WEEK'S FOCUS

TO DO LIST

PRIORITY

DUE

WEEK OF:

MONDAY	TUESDAY	WEDNESDAY	THURSDAY
MEALS	MEALS	MEALS	MEALS

PERSONAL TO DO LIST:

_____
_____
_____
_____
_____

WORK TO DO LIST:

_____
_____
_____
_____
_____

FRIDAY	SATURDAY	SUNDAY	THIS WEEK'S REMINDERS:
MEALS	MEALS	MEALS	

NOTES:

WEEKLY BUDGET

WEEK OF:

INCOME

Source	Estimated	Actual

SAVINGS

Account	Amount	+/-	Balance

DEBT

Description	Deposit	Balance

EXPENSES

Expense	Amount	Category

NOTES

WEEKLY

Total Income	
Total Debt	
Total Savings	
Total Expenses	

WEEKLY TO DO LIST

THIS WEEK'S FOCUS

TO DO LIST

PRIORITY

DUE

WEEK OF:

MONDAY	TUESDAY	WEDNESDAY	THURSDAY
MEALS	MEALS	MEALS	MEALS

PERSONAL TO DO LIST:

WORK TO DO LIST:

FRIDAY	SATURDAY	SUNDAY
MEALS	MEALS	MEALS

_____
_____
_____
_____
_____
_____
_____
_____
_____
_____
_____
_____
_____
_____
_____
_____
_____
_____
_____

NOTES:

WEEKLY BUDGET

WEEK OF:

INCOME

Source	Estimated	Actual

SAVINGS

Account	Amount	+/-	Balance

DEBT

Description	Deposit	Balance

EXPENSES

Expense	Amount	Category

NOTES

WEEKLY

Total Income	
Total Debt	
Total Savings	
Total Expenses	

WEEKLY TO DO LIST

TO DO LIST

PRIORITY

DUE

WEEK OF:

MONDAY	TUESDAY	WEDNESDAY	THURSDAY

MEALS   MEALS   MEALS   MEALS

PERSONAL TO DO LIST:

WORK TO DO LIST:

FRIDAY	SATURDAY	SUNDAY	THIS WEEK'S REMINDERS:
MEALS	MEALS	MEALS	

NOTES:

WEEKLY BUDGET

W E E K   O F :

INCOME

Source	Estimated	Actual

EXPENSES

Expense	Amount	Category

SAVINGS

Account	Amount	+/-	Balance

DEBT

Description	Deposit	Balance

NOTES

WEEKLY

Total Income	
Total Debt	
Total Savings	
Total Expenses	

WEEKLY TO DO LIST

THIS WEEK'S FOCUS

TO DO LIST

PRIORITY

DUE

WEEK OF:

MONDAY	TUESDAY	WEDNESDAY	THURSDAY
MEALS	MEALS	MEALS	MEALS

PERSONAL TO DO LIST:

_____
_____
_____
_____
_____

WORK TO DO LIST:

_____
_____
_____
_____
_____

FRIDAY	SATURDAY	SUNDAY	THIS WEEK'S REMINDERS:
MEALS	MEALS	MEALS	

NOTES:

GOALS UPDATE

MONTHLY OVERVIEW

SAVINGS

DEBT

WINS

CHALLENGES

NOTES

MONTH OF

GOALS	MONDAY	TUESDAY	WEDNESDAY
TARGET			
ACTUAL			
TARGET			
ACTUAL			
TARGET			
ACTUAL			

HABIT TRACKER

HABIT	1	2	3	4	5	6	7	8	9	10	11	12	13	14	15	16	17	18	19	20	21	22	23	24	25	26	27	28	29	30	31

THURSDAY	FRIDAY	SATURDAY	SUNDAY

NOTES

WEEKLY BUDGET

WEEK OF:

INCOME

Source	Estimated	Actual

SAVINGS

Account	Amount	+/-	Balance

DEBT

Description	Deposit	Balance

EXPENSES

Expense	Amount	Category

NOTES

WEEKLY

Total Income	
Total Debt	
Total Savings	
Total Expenses	

WEEKLY TO DO LIST

THIS WEEK'S FOCUS

TO DO LIST

PRIORITY

DUE

WEEK OF:

MONDAY	TUESDAY	WEDNESDAY	THURSDAY

MEALS   MEALS   MEALS   MEALS

PERSONAL TO DO LIST: WORK TO DO LIST:

FRIDAY	SATURDAY	SUNDAY
MEALS	MEALS	MEALS

_____
_____
_____
_____
_____
_____
_____
_____
_____
_____
_____
_____
_____
_____
_____
_____
_____
_____
_____
_____

NOTES:

WEEKLY BUDGET

WEEK OF:

INCOME

Source	Estimated	Actual

EXPENSES

Expense	Amount	Category

SAVINGS

Account	Amount	+/-	Balance

DEBT

Description	Deposit	Balance

NOTES

WEEKLY

Total Income	
Total Debt	
Total Savings	
Total Expenses	

WEEKLY TO DO LIST

TO DO LIST

PRIORITY

DUE

WEEK OF:

MONDAY	TUESDAY	WEDNESDAY	THURSDAY
MEALS	MEALS	MEALS	MEALS

PERSONAL TO DO LIST:

WORK TO DO LIST:

FRIDAY	SATURDAY	SUNDAY	THIS WEEK'S REMINDERS:
MEALS	MEALS	MEALS	

NOTES:

WEEKLY BUDGET

WEEK OF:

INCOME

Source	Estimated	Actual

SAVINGS

Account	Amount	+/-	Balance

DEBT

Description	Deposit	Balance

WEEKLY

Total Income	
Total Debt	
Total Savings	
Total Expenses	

EXPENSES

Expense	Amount	Category

NOTES

WEEKLY TO DO LIST

TO DO LIST

PRIORITY

DUE

WEEK OF:

MONDAY	TUESDAY	WEDNESDAY	THURSDAY

MEALS   MEALS   MEALS   MEALS

PERSONAL TO DO LIST:

_____
_____
_____
_____
_____

WORK TO DO LIST:

_____
_____
_____
_____
_____

FRIDAY	SATURDAY	SUNDAY
MEALS	MEALS	MEALS

NOTES:

WEEKLY BUDGET

WEEK OF:

INCOME

Source	Estimated	Actual

SAVINGS

Account	Amount	+/-	Balance

DEBT

Description	Deposit	Balance

WEEKLY

Total Income	
Total Debt	
Total Savings	
Total Expenses	

EXPENSES

Expense	Amount	Category

NOTES

WEEKLY TO DO LIST

THIS WEEK'S FOCUS

TO DO LIST

PRIORITY

DUE

WEEK OF:

MONDAY	TUESDAY	WEDNESDAY	THURSDAY

MEALS   MEALS   MEALS   MEALS

PERSONAL TO DO LIST:

_____
_____
_____
_____
_____

WORK TO DO LIST:

_____
_____
_____
_____
_____

FRIDAY	SATURDAY	SUNDAY	THIS WEEK'S REMINDERS:
MEALS	MEALS	MEALS	

NOTES:

GOALS UPDATE

MONTHLY OVERVIEW

SAVINGS

DEBT

WINS

CHALLENGES

NOTES

MONTH OF

GOALS	MONDAY	TUESDAY	WEDNESDAY
TARGET			
ACTUAL			
TARGET			
ACTUAL			
TARGET			
ACTUAL			

HABIT TRACKER

HABIT	1	2	3	4	5	6	7	8	9	10	11	12	13	14	15	16	17	18	19	20	21	22	23	24	25	26	27	28	29	30	31

THURSDAY	FRIDAY	SATURDAY	SUNDAY

NOTES

WEEKLY BUDGET

WEEK OF:

INCOME

Source	Estimated	Actual

SAVINGS

Account	Amount	+/-	Balance

DEBT

Description	Deposit	Balance

WEEKLY

Total Income	
Total Debt	
Total Savings	
Total Expenses	

EXPENSES

Expense	Amount	Category

NOTES

WEEKLY TO DO LIST

TO DO LIST

PRIORITY

DUE

WEEK OF:

MONDAY	TUESDAY	WEDNESDAY	THURSDAY
MEALS	MEALS	MEALS	MEALS

PERSONAL TO DO LIST:

_____
_____
_____
_____
_____

WORK TO DO LIST:

_____
_____
_____
_____
_____

FRIDAY	SATURDAY	SUNDAY	THIS WEEK'S REMINDERS:

MEALS   MEALS   MEALS

NOTES:

WEEKLY BUDGET

WEEK OF:

INCOME

Source	Estimated	Actual

SAVINGS

Account	Amount	+/-	Balance

DEBT

Description	Deposit	Balance

WEEKLY

Total Income	
Total Debt	
Total Savings	
Total Expenses	

EXPENSES

Expense	Amount	Category

NOTES

WEEKLY TO DO LIST

TO DO LIST

PRIORITY

DUE

WEEK OF:

MONDAY	TUESDAY	WEDNESDAY	THURSDAY
MEALS	MEALS	MEALS	MEALS

PERSONAL TO DO LIST:

_____

_____

_____

_____

_____

WORK TO DO LIST:

_____

_____

_____

_____

_____

FRIDAY	SATURDAY	SUNDAY	THIS WEEK'S REMINDERS:
MEALS	MEALS	MEALS	

NOTES:

WEEKLY BUDGET

W E E K   O F :

I N C O M E

Source	Estimated	Actual

S A V I N G S

Account	Amount	+/-	Balance

D E B T

Description	Deposit	Balance

W E E K L Y

Total Income	
Total Debt	
Total Savings	
Total Expenses	

E X P E N S E S

Expense	Amount	Category

NOTES

WEEKLY TO DO LIST

THIS WEEK'S FOCUS

TO DO LIST

PRIORITY

DUE

WEEK OF:

MONDAY	TUESDAY	WEDNESDAY	THURSDAY
MEALS	MEALS	MEALS	MEALS

PERSONAL TO DO LIST:

_____
_____
_____
_____
_____

WORK TO DO LIST:

_____
_____
_____
_____
_____

FRIDAY	SATURDAY	SUNDAY	THIS WEEK'S REMINDERS:
MEALS	MEALS	MEALS	

NOTES:

WEEKLY BUDGET

WEEK OF:

INCOME

Source	Estimated	Actual

EXPENSES

Expense	Amount	Category

SAVINGS

Account	Amount	+/-	Balance

DEBT

Description	Deposit	Balance

NOTES

WEEKLY

Total Income	
Total Debt	
Total Savings	
Total Expenses	

WEEKLY TO DO LIST

TO DO LIST

PRIORITY

DUE

WEEK OF:

MONDAY	TUESDAY	WEDNESDAY	THURSDAY
MEALS	MEALS	MEALS	MEALS

PERSONAL TO DO LIST:

WORK TO DO LIST:

FRIDAY	SATURDAY	SUNDAY	THIS WEEK'S REMINDERS:
MEALS	MEALS	MEALS	

NOTES:

GOALS UPDATE

MONTHLY OVERVIEW

SAVINGS

DEBT

WINS

CHALLENGES

NOTES

MONTH OF

GOALS	MONDAY	TUESDAY	WEDNESDAY
TARGET			
ACTUAL			
TARGET			
ACTUAL			
TARGET			
ACTUAL			

HABIT TRACKER

HABIT	1	2	3	4	5	6	7	8	9	10	11	12	13	14	15	16	17	18	19	20	21	22	23	24	25	26	27	28	29	30	31

THURSDAY	FRIDAY	SATURDAY	SUNDAY

NOTES

WEEKLY BUDGET

WEEK OF:

INCOME

Source	Estimated	Actual

SAVINGS

Account	Amount	+/-	Balance

DEBT

Description	Deposit	Balance

WEEKLY

Total Income	
Total Debt	
Total Savings	
Total Expenses	

EXPENSES

Expense	Amount	Category

NOTES

WEEKLY TO DO LIST

THIS WEEK'S FOCUS

TO DO LIST

PRIORITY

DUE

WEEK OF:

MONDAY	TUESDAY	WEDNESDAY	THURSDAY
MEALS	MEALS	MEALS	MEALS

PERSONAL TO DO LIST:

_____

_____

_____

_____

_____

WORK TO DO LIST:

_____

_____

_____

_____

_____

FRIDAY	SATURDAY	SUNDAY
MEALS	MEALS	MEALS

_____
_____
_____
_____
_____
_____
_____
_____
_____
_____
_____
_____
_____
_____
_____
_____
_____
_____
_____
_____
_____
_____

NOTES:

WEEKLY BUDGET

WEEK OF:

INCOME

Source	Estimated	Actual

SAVINGS

Account	Amount	+/-	Balance

DEBT

Description	Deposit	Balance

WEEKLY

Total Income	
Total Debt	
Total Savings	
Total Expenses	

EXPENSES

Expense	Amount	Category

NOTES

WEEKLY TO DO LIST

TO DO LIST

PRIORITY

DUE

WEEK OF:

MONDAY	TUESDAY	WEDNESDAY	THURSDAY

MEALS   MEALS   MEALS   MEALS

PERSONAL TO DO LIST: WORK TO DO LIST:

FRIDAY	SATURDAY	SUNDAY
MEALS	MEALS	MEALS

THIS WEEK'S REMINDERS:

_____
_____
_____
_____
_____
_____
_____
_____
_____
_____
_____
_____
_____
_____
_____
_____
_____
_____
_____

NOTES:

WEEKLY BUDGET

WEEK OF:

INCOME

Source	Estimated	Actual

SAVINGS

Account	Amount	+/-	Balance

DEBT

Description	Deposit	Balance

EXPENSES

Expense	Amount	Category

NOTES

WEEKLY

Total Income	
Total Debt	
Total Savings	
Total Expenses	

WEEKLY TO DO LIST

TO DO LIST

PRIORITY

DUE

WEEK OF:

MONDAY	TUESDAY	WEDNESDAY	THURSDAY

MEALS   MEALS   MEALS   MEALS

PERSONAL TO DO LIST:

_____
_____
_____
_____
_____

WORK TO DO LIST:

_____
_____
_____
_____
_____

FRIDAY	SATURDAY	SUNDAY
MEALS	MEALS	MEALS

THIS WEEK'S REMINDERS:

_____
_____
_____
_____
_____
_____
_____
_____
_____
_____
_____
_____
_____
_____
_____
_____
_____
_____
_____
_____

NOTES:

WEEKLY BUDGET

WEEK OF:

INCOME

Source	Estimated	Actual

SAVINGS

Account	Amount	+/-	Balance

DEBT

Description	Deposit	Balance

WEEKLY

Total Income	
Total Debt	
Total Savings	
Total Expenses	

EXPENSES

Expense	Amount	Category

NOTES

WEEKLY TO DO LIST

TO DO LIST

PRIORITY

DUE

WEEK OF:

MONDAY	TUESDAY	WEDNESDAY	THURSDAY
MEALS	MEALS	MEALS	MEALS

PERSONAL TO DO LIST:

_____
_____
_____
_____
_____

WORK TO DO LIST:

_____
_____
_____
_____
_____

FRIDAY	SATURDAY	SUNDAY	THIS WEEK'S REMINDERS:

MEALS   MEALS   MEALS

NOTES:

GOALS UPDATE

MONTHLY OVERVIEW

SAVINGS

DEBT

WINS

CHALLENGES

NOTES

MONTH OF

GOALS	MONDAY	TUESDAY	WEDNESDAY
TARGET			
ACTUAL			
TARGET			
ACTUAL			
TARGET			
ACTUAL			

HABIT TRACKER

HABIT	1	2	3	4	5	6	7	8	9	10	11	12	13	14	15	16	17	18	19	20	21	22	23	24	25	26	27	28	29	30	31

THURSDAY	FRIDAY	SATURDAY	SUNDAY

NOTES

WEEKLY BUDGET

WEEK OF:

INCOME

Source	Estimated	Actual

SAVINGS

Account	Amount	+/-	Balance

DEBT

Description	Deposit	Balance

EXPENSES

Expense	Amount	Category

NOTES

WEEKLY

Total Income	
Total Debt	
Total Savings	
Total Expenses	

WEEKLY TO DO LIST

TO DO LIST

PRIORITY

DUE

WEEK OF:

MONDAY	TUESDAY	WEDNESDAY	THURSDAY
MEALS	MEALS	MEALS	MEALS

PERSONAL TO DO LIST:

_____
_____
_____
_____
_____
_____

WORK TO DO LIST:

_____
_____
_____
_____
_____
_____

FRIDAY	SATURDAY	SUNDAY	THIS WEEK'S REMINDERS:
MEALS	MEALS	MEALS	

NOTES:

WEEKLY BUDGET

WEEK OF:

INCOME

Source	Estimated	Actual

SAVINGS

Account	Amount	+/-	Balance

DEBT

Description	Deposit	Balance

WEEKLY

Total Income	
Total Debt	
Total Savings	
Total Expenses	

EXPENSES

Expense	Amount	Category

NOTES

WEEKLY TO DO LIST

TO DO LIST

PRIORITY

DUE

WEEK OF:

MONDAY	TUESDAY	WEDNESDAY	THURSDAY
MEALS	MEALS	MEALS	MEALS

PERSONAL TO DO LIST:

_____
_____
_____
_____
_____
_____

WORK TO DO LIST:

_____
_____
_____
_____
_____
_____

FRIDAY	SATURDAY	SUNDAY	THIS WEEK'S REMINDERS:
MEALS	MEALS	MEALS	

NOTES:

WEEKLY BUDGET

WEEK OF:

INCOME

Source	Estimated	Actual

SAVINGS

Account	Amount	+/-	Balance

DEBT

Description	Deposit	Balance

EXPENSES

Expense	Amount	Category

NOTES

WEEKLY

Total Income	
Total Debt	
Total Savings	
Total Expenses	

WEEKLY TO DO LIST

THIS WEEK'S FOCUS

TO DO LIST

PRIORITY

DUE

WEEK OF:

MONDAY	TUESDAY	WEDNESDAY	THURSDAY
MEALS	MEALS	MEALS	MEALS

PERSONAL TO DO LIST:

_____
_____
_____
_____
_____

WORK TO DO LIST:

_____
_____
_____
_____
_____

FRIDAY	SATURDAY	SUNDAY	THIS WEEK'S REMINDERS:
MEALS	MEALS	MEALS	

NOTES:

WEEKLY BUDGET

WEEK OF:

INCOME

Source	Estimated	Actual

SAVINGS

Account	Amount	+/-	Balance

DEBT

Description	Deposit	Balance

WEEKLY

Total Income	
Total Debt	
Total Savings	
Total Expenses	

EXPENSES

Expense	Amount	Category

NOTES

WEEKLY TO DO LIST

TO DO LIST

PRIORITY

DUE

WEEK OF:

MONDAY	TUESDAY	WEDNESDAY	THURSDAY

MEALS   MEALS   MEALS   MEALS

PERSONAL TO DO LIST:

_____

_____

_____

_____

_____

WORK TO DO LIST:

_____

_____

_____

_____

_____

FRIDAY	SATURDAY	SUNDAY	THIS WEEK'S REMINDERS:
MEALS	MEALS	MEALS	

NOTES:

GOALS UPDATE

MONTHLY OVERVIEW

SAVINGS

DEBT

WINS

CHALLENGES

NOTES

MONTH OF

GOALS	MONDAY	TUESDAY	WEDNESDAY
TARGET			
ACTUAL			
TARGET			
ACTUAL			
TARGET			
ACTUAL			

HABIT TRACKER

HABIT	1	2	3	4	5	6	7	8	9	10	11	12	13	14	15	16	17	18	19	20	21	22	23	24	25	26	27	28	29	30	31

THURSDAY	FRIDAY	SATURDAY	SUNDAY

NOTES

WEEKLY BUDGET

W E E K   O F :

I N C O M E

Source	Estimated	Actual

S A V I N G S

Account	Amount	+/-	Balance

D E B T

Description	Deposit	Balance

W E E K L Y

Total Income	
Total Debt	
Total Savings	
Total Expenses	

E X P E N S E S

Expense	Amount	Category

NOTES

WEEKLY TO DO LIST

THIS WEEK'S FOCUS

TO DO LIST

PRIORITY

DUE

WEEK OF:

MONDAY	TUESDAY	WEDNESDAY	THURSDAY
MEALS	MEALS	MEALS	MEALS

PERSONAL TO DO LIST:

_____

_____

_____

_____

_____

_____

WORK TO DO LIST:

_____

_____

_____

_____

_____

_____

FRIDAY	SATURDAY	SUNDAY
MEALS	MEALS	MEALS

THIS WEEK'S REMINDERS:

_____
_____
_____
_____
_____
_____
_____
_____
_____
_____
_____
_____
_____
_____
_____
_____
_____
_____

NOTES:

WEEKLY BUDGET

WEEK OF:

INCOME

Source	Estimated	Actual

SAVINGS

Account	Amount	+/-	Balance

DEBT

Description	Deposit	Balance

WEEKLY

Total Income	
Total Debt	
Total Savings	
Total Expenses	

EXPENSES

Expense	Amount	Category

NOTES

WEEKLY TO DO LIST

THIS WEEK'S FOCUS

TO DO LIST	PRIORITY

DUE

WEEK OF:

MONDAY	TUESDAY	WEDNESDAY	THURSDAY
MEALS	MEALS	MEALS	MEALS

PERSONAL TO DO LIST:

_____
_____
_____
_____
_____

WORK TO DO LIST:

_____
_____
_____
_____
_____

FRIDAY	SATURDAY	SUNDAY	THIS WEEK'S REMINDERS:
MEALS	MEALS	MEALS	

NOTES:

WEEKLY BUDGET

WEEK OF:

INCOME

Source	Estimated	Actual

SAVINGS

Account	Amount	+/-	Balance

DEBT

Description	Deposit	Balance

WEEKLY

Total Income	
Total Debt	
Total Savings	
Total Expenses	

EXPENSES

Expense	Amount	Category

NOTES

WEEKLY TO DO LIST

TO DO LIST

PRIORITY

DUE

WEEK OF:

MONDAY	TUESDAY	WEDNESDAY	THURSDAY
MEALS	MEALS	MEALS	MEALS

PERSONAL TO DO LIST:

WORK TO DO LIST:

FRIDAY	SATURDAY	SUNDAY	THIS WEEK'S REMINDERS:

MEALS   MEALS   MEALS

NOTES:

WEEKLY BUDGET

WEEK OF:

INCOME

Source	Estimated	Actual

SAVINGS

Account	Amount	+/-	Balance

DEBT

Description	Deposit	Balance

WEEKLY

Total Income	
Total Debt	
Total Savings	
Total Expenses	

EXPENSES

Expense	Amount	Category

NOTES

WEEKLY TO DO LIST

TO DO LIST

PRIORITY

DUE

WEEK OF:

MONDAY	TUESDAY	WEDNESDAY	THURSDAY
MEALS	MEALS	MEALS	MEALS

PERSONAL TO DO LIST:

_____
_____
_____
_____
_____

WORK TO DO LIST:

_____
_____
_____
_____
_____

FRIDAY	SATURDAY	SUNDAY	THIS WEEK'S REMINDERS:
MEALS	MEALS	MEALS	

NOTES:

GOALS UPDATE

MONTHLY OVERVIEW

SAVINGS

DEBT

WINS

CHALLENGES

NOTES

MONTH OF

GOALS	MONDAY	TUESDAY	WEDNESDAY
TARGET			
ACTUAL			
TARGET			
ACTUAL			
TARGET			
ACTUAL			

HABIT TRACKER

HABIT	1 2 3 4 5 6 7 8 9 10 11 12 13 14 15 16 17 18 19 20 21 22 23 24 25 26 27 28 29 30 31

THURSDAY	FRIDAY	SATURDAY	SUNDAY

NOTES

WEEKLY BUDGET

W E E K   O F :

I N C O M E

Source	Estimated	Actual

S A V I N G S

Account	Amount	+/-	Balance

D E B T

Description	Deposit	Balance

W E E K L Y

Total Income	
Total Debt	
Total Savings	
Total Expenses	

E X P E N S E S

Expense	Amount	Category

NOTES

WEEKLY TO DO LIST

TO DO LIST

PRIORITY

DUE

WEEK OF:

MONDAY	TUESDAY	WEDNESDAY	THURSDAY

MEALS　　　　MEALS　　　　MEALS　　　　MEALS

PERSONAL TO DO LIST:

_____

_____

_____

_____

_____

WORK TO DO LIST:

_____

_____

_____

_____

_____

FRIDAY	SATURDAY	SUNDAY	THIS WEEK'S REMINDERS:
MEALS	MEALS	MEALS	

NOTES:

WEEKLY BUDGET

WEEK OF:

INCOME

Source	Estimated	Actual

SAVINGS

Account	Amount	+/-	Balance

DEBT

Description	Deposit	Balance

WEEKLY

Total Income	
Total Debt	
Total Savings	
Total Expenses	

EXPENSES

Expense	Amount	Category

NOTES

WEEKLY TO DO LIST

THIS WEEK'S FOCUS

TO DO LIST

PRIORITY

DUE

WEEK OF:

MONDAY	TUESDAY	WEDNESDAY	THURSDAY
MEALS	MEALS	MEALS	MEALS

PERSONAL TO DO LIST:

_____
_____
_____
_____
_____

WORK TO DO LIST:

_____
_____
_____
_____
_____

FRIDAY	SATURDAY	SUNDAY	THIS WEEK'S REMINDERS:
MEALS	MEALS	MEALS	

NOTES:

WEEKLY BUDGET

WEEK OF:

INCOME

Source	Estimated	Actual

SAVINGS

Account	Amount	+/-	Balance

DEBT

Description	Deposit	Balance

WEEKLY

Total Income	
Total Debt	
Total Savings	
Total Expenses	

EXPENSES

Expense	Amount	Category

NOTES

WEEKLY TO DO LIST

TO DO LIST

PRIORITY

DUE

WEEK OF:

MONDAY	TUESDAY	WEDNESDAY	THURSDAY
MEALS	MEALS	MEALS	MEALS

PERSONAL TO DO LIST:

_____

_____

_____

_____

_____

WORK TO DO LIST:

_____

_____

_____

_____

_____

FRIDAY	SATURDAY	SUNDAY	THIS WEEK'S REMINDERS:
MEALS	MEALS	MEALS	

NOTES:

WEEKLY BUDGET

W E E K   O F :

INCOME

Source	Estimated	Actual

SAVINGS

Account	Amount	+/-	Balance

DEBT

Description	Deposit	Balance

WEEKLY

Total Income	
Total Debt	
Total Savings	
Total Expenses	

EXPENSES

Expense	Amount	Category

NOTES

WEEKLY TO DO LIST

THIS WEEK'S FOCUS

TO DO LIST

PRIORITY

DUE

WEEK OF:

MONDAY	TUESDAY	WEDNESDAY	THURSDAY
MEALS	MEALS	MEALS	MEALS

PERSONAL TO DO LIST:

WORK TO DO LIST:

FRIDAY	SATURDAY	SUNDAY	THIS WEEK'S REMINDERS:

MEALS   MEALS   MEALS

NOTES:

GOALS UPDATE

MONTHLY OVERVIEW

SAVINGS

DEBT

WINS

CHALLENGES

NOTES

MONTH OF

GOALS	MONDAY	TUESDAY	WEDNESDAY
TARGET ACTUAL			
TARGET ACTUAL			
TARGET ACTUAL			

HABIT TRACKER

HABIT	1 2 3 4 5 6 7 8 9 10 11 12 13 14 15 16 17 18 19 20 21 22 23 24 25 26 27 28 29 30 31

THURSDAY	FRIDAY	SATURDAY	SUNDAY

NOTES

WEEKLY BUDGET

WEEK OF:

INCOME

Source	Estimated	Actual

SAVINGS

Account	Amount	+/-	Balance

DEBT

Description	Deposit	Balance

WEEKLY

Total Income	
Total Debt	
Total Savings	
Total Expenses	

EXPENSES

Expense	Amount	Category

NOTES

WEEKLY TO DO LIST

TO DO LIST

PRIORITY

DUE

WEEK OF:

MONDAY	TUESDAY	WEDNESDAY	THURSDAY
MEALS	MEALS	MEALS	MEALS

PERSONAL TO DO LIST:

_____
_____
_____
_____
_____

WORK TO DO LIST:

_____
_____
_____
_____
_____

FRIDAY	SATURDAY	SUNDAY
MEALS	MEALS	MEALS

NOTES:

WEEKLY BUDGET

WEEK OF:

INCOME

Source	Estimated	Actual

SAVINGS

Account	Amount	+/-	Balance

DEBT

Description	Deposit	Balance

WEEKLY

Total Income	
Total Debt	
Total Savings	
Total Expenses	

EXPENSES

Expense	Amount	Category

NOTES

WEEKLY TO DO LIST

THIS WEEK'S FOCUS

TO DO LIST

PRIORITY

DUE

WEEK OF:

MONDAY	TUESDAY	WEDNESDAY	THURSDAY
MEALS	MEALS	MEALS	MEALS

PERSONAL TO DO LIST:

_____
_____
_____
_____
_____
_____

WORK TO DO LIST:

_____
_____
_____
_____
_____
_____

FRIDAY	SATURDAY	SUNDAY
MEALS	MEALS	MEALS

NOTES:

WEEKLY BUDGET

WEEK OF:

INCOME

Source	Estimated	Actual

SAVINGS

Account	Amount	+/-	Balance

DEBT

Description	Deposit	Balance

EXPENSES

Expense	Amount	Category

NOTES

WEEKLY

Total Income	
Total Debt	
Total Savings	
Total Expenses	

WEEKLY TO DO LIST

THIS WEEK'S FOCUS

TO DO LIST	PRIORITY

DUE

WEEK OF:

MONDAY	TUESDAY	WEDNESDAY	THURSDAY
MEALS	MEALS	MEALS	MEALS

PERSONAL TO DO LIST:

_____
_____
_____
_____
_____

WORK TO DO LIST:

_____
_____
_____
_____
_____

FRIDAY	SATURDAY	SUNDAY
MEALS	MEALS	MEALS

NOTES:

WEEKLY BUDGET

WEEK OF:

INCOME

Source	Estimated	Actual

SAVINGS

Account	Amount	+/-	Balance

DEBT

Description	Deposit	Balance

WEEKLY

Total Income	
Total Debt	
Total Savings	
Total Expenses	

EXPENSES

Expense	Amount	Category

NOTES

WEEKLY TO DO LIST

THIS WEEK'S FOCUS

TO DO LIST

PRIORITY

DUE

WEEK OF:

MONDAY	TUESDAY	WEDNESDAY	THURSDAY
MEALS	MEALS	MEALS	MEALS

PERSONAL TO DO LIST:

_____

_____

_____

_____

_____

WORK TO DO LIST:

_____

_____

_____

_____

_____

FRIDAY	SATURDAY	SUNDAY
MEALS	MEALS	MEALS

THIS WEEK'S REMINDERS:

_____
_____
_____
_____
_____
_____
_____
_____
_____
_____
_____
_____
_____
_____
_____
_____
_____
_____
_____
_____
_____

NOTES:

GOALS UPDATE

MONTHLY OVERVIEW

SAVINGS

DEBT

WINS

CHALLENGES

NOTES

MONTH OF

GOALS	MONDAY	TUESDAY	WEDNESDAY
TARGET			
ACTUAL			
TARGET			
ACTUAL			
TARGET			
ACTUAL			

HABIT TRACKER

HABIT	1 2 3 4 5 6 7 8 9 10 11 12 13 14 15 16 17 18 19 20 21 22 23 24 25 26 27 28 29 30 31

THURSDAY	FRIDAY	SATURDAY	SUNDAY

NOTES

WEEKLY BUDGET

WEEK OF:

INCOME

Source	Estimated	Actual

SAVINGS

Account	Amount	+/-	Balance

DEBT

Description	Deposit	Balance

WEEKLY

Total Income	
Total Debt	
Total Savings	
Total Expenses	

EXPENSES

Expense	Amount	Category

NOTES

WEEKLY TO DO LIST

THIS WEEK'S FOCUS

TO DO LIST

PRIORITY

DUE

WEEK OF:

MONDAY	TUESDAY	WEDNESDAY	THURSDAY
MEALS	MEALS	MEALS	MEALS

PERSONAL TO DO LIST:

WORK TO DO LIST:

FRIDAY	SATURDAY	SUNDAY
MEALS	MEALS	MEALS

NOTES:

WEEKLY BUDGET

W E E K   O F :

I N C O M E

Source	Estimated	Actual

S A V I N G S

Account	Amount	+/-	Balance

D E B T

Description	Deposit	Balance

W E E K L Y

Total Income	
Total Debt	
Total Savings	
Total Expenses	

E X P E N S E S

Expense	Amount	Category

NOTES

WEEKLY TO DO LIST

THIS WEEK'S FOCUS

TO DO LIST

PRIORITY

DUE

WEEK OF:

MONDAY	TUESDAY	WEDNESDAY	THURSDAY
MEALS	MEALS	MEALS	MEALS

PERSONAL TO DO LIST:

_____

_____

_____

_____

_____

WORK TO DO LIST:

_____

_____

_____

_____

_____

FRIDAY	SATURDAY	SUNDAY
MEALS	MEALS	MEALS

NOTES:

WEEKLY BUDGET

WEEK OF:

INCOME

Source	Estimated	Actual

SAVINGS

Account	Amount	+/-	Balance

DEBT

Description	Deposit	Balance

WEEKLY

Total Income	
Total Debt	
Total Savings	
Total Expenses	

EXPENSES

Expense	Amount	Category

NOTES

WEEKLY TO DO LIST

THIS WEEK'S FOCUS

TO DO LIST

PRIORITY

DUE

WEEK OF:

MONDAY	TUESDAY	WEDNESDAY	THURSDAY
MEALS	MEALS	MEALS	MEALS

PERSONAL TO DO LIST:

_____

_____

_____

_____

_____

WORK TO DO LIST:

_____

_____

_____

_____

_____

FRIDAY	SATURDAY	SUNDAY	THIS WEEK'S REMINDERS:
MEALS	MEALS	MEALS	

NOTES:

WEEKLY BUDGET

W E E K O F :

INCOME

Source	Estimated	Actual

SAVINGS

Account	Amount	+/-	Balance

DEBT

Description	Deposit	Balance

WEEKLY

Total Income	
Total Debt	
Total Savings	
Total Expenses	

EXPENSES

Expense	Amount	Category

NOTES

WEEKLY TO DO LIST

TO DO LIST

PRIORITY

DUE

WEEK OF:

MONDAY	TUESDAY	WEDNESDAY	THURSDAY
MEALS	MEALS	MEALS	MEALS

PERSONAL TO DO LIST:

_____
_____
_____
_____
_____

WORK TO DO LIST:

_____
_____
_____
_____
_____

FRIDAY	SATURDAY	SUNDAY	THIS WEEK'S REMINDERS:
MEALS	MEALS	MEALS	

NOTES:

GOALS UPDATE

MONTHLY OVERVIEW

SAVINGS

DEBT

WINS

CHALLENGES

NOTES

MONTH OF

GOALS	MONDAY	TUESDAY	WEDNESDAY
TARGET			
ACTUAL			
TARGET			
ACTUAL			
TARGET			
ACTUAL			

HABIT TRACKER

HABIT	1 2 3 4 5 6 7 8 9 10 11 12 13 14 15 16 17 18 19 20 21 22 23 24 25 26 27 28 29 30 31

THURSDAY	FRIDAY	SATURDAY	SUNDAY

NOTES

WEEKLY BUDGET

WEEK OF:

INCOME

Source	Estimated	Actual

SAVINGS

Account	Amount	+/-	Balance

DEBT

Description	Deposit	Balance

WEEKLY

Total Income	
Total Debt	
Total Savings	
Total Expenses	

EXPENSES

Expense	Amount	Category

NOTES

WEEKLY TO DO LIST

THIS WEEK'S FOCUS

TO DO LIST

PRIORITY

DUE

WEEK OF:

MONDAY	TUESDAY	WEDNESDAY	THURSDAY
MEALS	MEALS	MEALS	MEALS

PERSONAL TO DO LIST:

_____

_____

_____

_____

_____

WORK TO DO LIST:

_____

_____

_____

_____

_____

FRIDAY	SATURDAY	SUNDAY
MEALS	MEALS	MEALS

THIS WEEK'S REMINDERS:

NOTES:

WEEKLY BUDGET

WEEK OF:

INCOME

Source	Estimated	Actual

SAVINGS

Account	Amount	+/-	Balance

DEBT

Description	Deposit	Balance

WEEKLY

Total Income	
Total Debt	
Total Savings	
Total Expenses	

EXPENSES

Expense	Amount	Category

NOTES

WEEKLY TO DO LIST

THIS WEEK'S FOCUS

TO DO LIST

PRIORITY

DUE

WEEK OF:

MONDAY	TUESDAY	WEDNESDAY	THURSDAY
MEALS	MEALS	MEALS	MEALS

PERSONAL TO DO LIST:

_____
_____
_____
_____
_____

WORK TO DO LIST:

_____
_____
_____
_____
_____

FRIDAY	SATURDAY	SUNDAY	THIS WEEK'S REMINDERS:
MEALS	MEALS	MEALS	

NOTES:

WEEKLY BUDGET

W E E K   O F :

I N C O M E

Source	Estimated	Actual

S A V I N G S

Account	Amount	+/-	Balance

D E B T

Description	Deposit	Balance

W E E K L Y

Total Income	
Total Debt	
Total Savings	
Total Expenses	

E X P E N S E S

Expense	Amount	Category

NOTES

WEEKLY TO DO LIST

THIS WEEK'S FOCUS

TO DO LIST	PRIORITY

DUE

WEEK OF:

MONDAY	TUESDAY	WEDNESDAY	THURSDAY
MEALS	MEALS	MEALS	MEALS

PERSONAL TO DO LIST:

_____
_____
_____
_____
_____
_____

WORK TO DO LIST:

_____
_____
_____
_____
_____
_____

FRIDAY	SATURDAY	SUNDAY
MEALS	MEALS	MEALS

NOTES:

WEEKLY BUDGET

WEEK OF:

INCOME

Source	Estimated	Actual

SAVINGS

Account	Amount	+/-	Balance

DEBT

Description	Deposit	Balance

WEEKLY

Total Income	
Total Debt	
Total Savings	
Total Expenses	

EXPENSES

Expense	Amount	Category

NOTES

WEEKLY TO DO LIST

THIS WEEK'S FOCUS

TO DO LIST

PRIORITY

DUE

WEEK OF:

MONDAY	TUESDAY	WEDNESDAY	THURSDAY
MEALS	MEALS	MEALS	MEALS

PERSONAL TO DO LIST:

_____
_____
_____
_____
_____
_____

WORK TO DO LIST:

_____
_____
_____
_____
_____
_____

FRIDAY	SATURDAY	SUNDAY
MEALS	MEALS	MEALS

_____
_____
_____
_____
_____
_____
_____
_____
_____
_____
_____
_____
_____
_____
_____
_____
_____
_____
_____
_____

NOTES:

GOALS UPDATE

MONTHLY OVERVIEW

SAVINGS

DEBT

WINS

CHALLENGES

NOTES

GOALS UPDATE

GOAL ONE

GOAL TWO

GOAL THREE

GOAL FOUR

YEARLY REFLECTION

NOTES

www.ingramcontent.com/pod-product-compliance
Lightning Source LLC
Chambersburg PA
CBHW040828300326
41914CB00059B/1291